GAM

Contents

Stories illustrated by Tom Percival and Steve May

In this story

 Rusty

 The children

Tricky words

- children
- football
- threw

Introduce these tricky words and help the reader when they come across them later!

Story starter

Rusty is a robot. He is old and rusty but he likes to help people. One day, Rusty saw two children in the park. Their football was stuck in a tree.

Rusty and the Football

"Help!" said the children.

"The football is in the tree," said the children.
"Can you help?"

4

"Yes, I can help,"
said Rusty.

Rusty got the football.

Rusty threw the football.

The football went in the mud.

The mud went on the children.

"Help!" said the children.

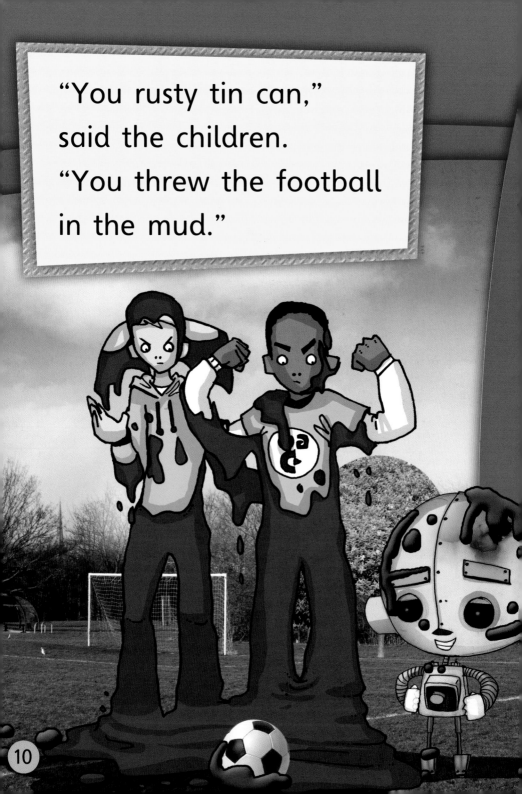

"You rusty tin can,"
said the children.
"You threw the football
in the mud."

"But I can help you,"
said Rusty.

Quiz

Text Detective

- Why did the children ask Rusty to help them?
- How did Rusty help in the end?
- Would you like to have a robot like Rusty?

Word Detective

Phonic Assessment: Initial phonemes

- Listen to the word 'yes'. What phoneme can you hear at the beginning? Write the letter.
- Listen to the word 'got'. What phoneme can you hear at the beginning? Write the letter.
- Listen to the word 'mud'. What phoneme can you hear at the beginning? Write the letter.

Super Speller

Can you spell these words from memory?

is   on   in

HA! HA! HA!

Q Why were the flies playing football in the saucer?

A Because they were playing for the cup.

13

In this story

 Lee

 Emma

Tricky words

- race
- faster

Introduce these tricky words and help the reader when they come across them later!

Story starter

Emma and Lee are twins. They are great friends but one twin is always trying to be better than the other twin. On Sports Day, the twins both wanted to win the running race.

The Race

"I will win the race,"
said Emma.
"I will win the race,"
said Lee.

"I can go faster than you," said Lee.

Emma ran and ran.

Lee ran and ran.

But Emma and Lee did not win the race.

"We did not win the race," said Emma.

"We will win this race," said Lee.

Emma and Lee ran and ran.

Emma and Lee did win the race!

Quiz

Text Detective

- Did Lee and Emma win the running race?
- Why were Lee and Emma good at the three-legged race?
- Do you like running races? What are you best at?

Word Detective

Phonic Assessment: Initial phonemes

- Listen to the word 'win'. What phoneme can you hear at the beginning? Write the letter.
- Listen to the word 'ran'. What phoneme can you hear at the beginning? Write the letter.
- Listen to the word 'not'. What phoneme can you hear at the beginning? Write the letter.

Super Speller

Can you spell these words from memory?

go   we   no

HA! HA! HA!

Q How do you start an onion race?

A Say, "Onion marks, get set, go!"